# THE NEW ILLUSTRATION

From the exhibition held at
**The Society of Illustrators
Museum of American Illustration**
128 East 63rd Street,
New York City

# THE NEW ILLUSTRATION

Published by Madison Square Press
for the Society of Illustrators

Associate Publisher, Simms Taback

**Madison Square Press, Inc.**
10 East 23rd Street, New York, N.Y. 10010

ISBN 0-942604-06-7
Library of Congress Catalog Card Number: 84-62355

Distributors to the trade
in the United States:
Robert Silver Associates
307 East 37th Street
New York, N.Y. 10016

Publisher:
Madison Square Press
10 East 23rd Street
New York, N.Y. 10010

Printed and bound in Korea
through Creative Graphics International Inc.

Design: Ross Design Associates, Inc.
**Cover Design: Bud Lavery**
**Cover Illustration: Lou Brooks/Michael Doret**
Interior: Mecca Culbert
Typography: I Claudia
Editor: Jill Bossert

Recently, a friend was turned down for an artist membership in the Museum of Modern Art because he was an illustrator.

These are the 1980s after all, and stone-age ideas seem to have a way of surfacing all over the place. Still, we get pretty surprised at such triviality, especially at a time when these distinctions have clearly broken down, and when the line between the "high" art of established museums and the aesthetic of everyday life as produced by the media is very fuzzy indeed.

At the same time, what was striking about The New Illustration exhibition was that elitest attitudes about illustration was being demolished. The "New" art) were being demolished. The "New" illustrators threw a pie in the face of accepted illustration and the rest of us were "unstuck" enough to be receptive to a newer conception. Better yet, the more or less traditional Society of Illustrators threw its arms open to it. Whether you hated The New Illustration or loved it, the important message for me was that a bridge was there when we needed it.

What sets illustrators apart from other practitioners, if anything, is that they are linked together by their own particular history. It's important, then, that we thank the Society of Illustrators and Society President, John Witt, for understanding this and making The New Illustration a reality.

**Simms Taback,** New York City, 1984

## Entry Description

The art world has always mirrored our times, but in spite of our economic woes, illustration today seems to be everywhere and more adventurous than ever. The premise of this show is that a different sensibility and a new direction in illustration has begun to define itself. It began with the rock album covers in the '70s and has developed through styles as diverse as nostalgic, punk, new wave or Bauhaus-revival. It's been influenced by Maxfield Parrish, cubism, '30s industrial design, Vargas, Disney, movie stars—styles from the deco '20s to the high-tech '80s. This show is an invitation to specially selected people involved in generating and executing this new illustration, but more important, we will look at what is fresh and interesting in American Illustration today.

## Terms and Conditions, Eligibility

Any illustrative work, whether published or unpublished, completed in the U.S. between Jan. 1, 1975 and July 30, 1982 was eligible for entry. There were no categories. Any work done for the print media, including work for advertising, editorial or promotional use, books, greeting cards, etc. was judged only on merit without any regard to its use or non-use.

**The Committee**

Simms Taback, Chairperson
Doug Johnson
Wilson McLean
Jim McMullan
Barbara Nessim

**The Jury**

Lou Brooks, Jury Chairperson, Illustrator
Brad Benedict, Editor
Carol Carson, Art Director
Michael Doret, Graphic Designer/Illustrator
Mare Earley, Art Director
Mick Haggerty, Illustrator
Ken Kneitel, Graphic Designer
Robert Risko, Illustrator
Laurie Rosenwald, Graphic Designer/Illustrator
Paula Scher, Art Director
Todd Schorr, Illustrator
Jim Wilson, Art Director/Illustrator

*THE NEW ILLUSTRATION: An invitation to enter a special juried exhibition of American illustration sponsored by the Society of Illustrators of New York.*

## With Special Thanks To:

Lou Brooks
Terry Brown
Carol Carson
Tom Cathey
Dorothy Chapman
Gerry Contreras
Sheila Debrettville
Mare Earley
Arpi Ermoyan
Dagmar Frinta
Mick Haggerty
Steve Heller
Walter Herdeg
Steve Hoffman
Rudolph Hoglund
D.K. Holland
Lily Hou
Karen Jacobson
Tibor Kalman
Paul Maringelli
Jerry McConnell
Jim McMullan
Barbara Nessim
Norma Pimsler
Don Ivan Punchatz
Laurie Rosenwald
Scarlett Letters, Inc.
Paula Scher
Todd Schorr
Mary Shanahan
Art Speigelman
Elwood Smith
The Three Stooges
Jim Wilson
Lloyd Ziff

## Call for Entry Poster
Illustration: Mick Haggerty
Design: Carol Carson
Typography: Scarlett Letters, Inc.

Brad Benedict and good friend
Todd Schorr having some fun in
the South Pacific.

## Passion and the New Illustration

**A**rt is a reflection of the society in which it is created. As I write this, I can't help hearing Albert Brooks ask himself: "Was that a cliché? No, it couldn't have been—everyone says it!"

Still, it is not an accident that what has come to be labeled as "The New Illustration" has emerged in post-Vietnam, post-Sesame Street, post-McDonald's America. The "Golden Age" of American illustration—the era dominated by *The Saturday Evening Post*, Maxfield Parrish, Norman Rockwell, et. al.— served to promote an idyllic version of the American Dream. It forged a cultural common denominator for a nation that was still provincial, small-scale, decentralized—and strikingly smug about its values, sensibilities and life-styles. The illustrations and commercial art of this period were meant to convey soothing, reassuring images.

By contrast, the "new" attitude in illustration is the hallmark of a generation seeking to stimulate, to grab attention and, occasionally, to shock. These commercial artists and art directors are eclectic in their techniques, media, influences, and visions. Yet they are linked by their shared faith in the power of highly personal images in an increasingly faceless society. They don't smooth over the rough corners of their subjects, whether products, personalities or places. The New Illustration has a definite edge to it. Sometimes the edge is expressed through irony, through turning familiar dimensions of the American Dream inside out or upside down, through brash colors, through exaggeration and very often

through humor. The humor is essential. It keeps self-righteousness and pretentiousness at a minimum, while highlighting the absurdity of so much of what passes as real life. More to the point, much of this kind of illustration is just plain fun.

In fact, it was their capacity to provoke laughter that first attracted me to these innovative artists. I respected "fine art" and enjoyed the illustrations of the "Golden Age," but I fell in love with the new generation and new spirit of commercial art and design. My desire to share my own delight and to help an overlooked group of talented artists gain the recognition they deserved led me to begin a series of creative enterprises.

Inspired by "Pop Art" and artists such as Andy Warhol, Roy Lichtenstein and Robert Rauschenberg, the new illustrators first had the freedom to "push the limits" and express themselves through rock concert posters and record industry art. Their work inspired my first book *Phonographics, Contemporary Album Cover Art*. It was only a small leap from there to the idea of popularizing this style of illustration through greeting cards and paper goods—that idea turned into Paper Moon Graphics. This was soon followed by several other books which brought together the best of this new art around a variety of themes.

Inevitably my passion for this artistic perspective found its realization in the development of a contemporary retail operation named Heaven. These West Coast stores give me free reign to merchandize the New Illustration as popular art in popular forms—T-shirts and clothing, shopping bags, postcards, posters, buttons, mugs, tinware, toys, food, etc.

Although difficult to define or pigeonhole, the New Illustration has already clearly made its mark and shows no sign of fading away. Personally, I'm delighted. My own enthusiasm remains strong.

Ironically, my one concern is that this genre of popular commercial art will become, well, too popular and commercial. The issue is one of standards, of quality, of purity. Admittedly, there is a fine line between "kitsch" and trash, between "cult" and crap, between "esoteric" and obscure and between "pop" and poop. Still, there is a line and the line is a real one that must be maintained. To paraphrase Mark Twain: You can never go wrong underestimating the taste of the American public. Perhaps the exhibition, publication and mass merchandising of the New Illustration will modify Mr. Twain's pronouncement and keep more people on the right side of that fine line.

It comes down to attitude and talent. It was a fresh, irreverent, joyful attitude that launched the New Illustration and that is precisely the attitude that will keep it afloat. It's an attitude well-represented by Martin Mull sneaking into the Boston Museum of Fine Arts and putting a sign on the men's room door declaring: "Wait, I'll be Art in a Minute!"

**Brad Benedict,** Los Angeles 1984

*Brad Benedict is co-founder of Paper Moon Graphics; his books include: Fame, Love: the Art of Romance, Cool Cats, The Blue Book and Fame II. His Heaven Stores have been dubbed, "the supermarket of pop culture" and "Woolworth's for the insane."*

# INTRODUCTION

**S**omething young and vigorous was happening in the world of illustration. It loomed on the horizon of the mid-'70s; then, picking up speed, it raced into the hearts, minds and paint pots of a new generation of illustrators and designers. It seemed obvious that a new attitude and a new sensibility was emerging. It revealed itself in an array of styles—everything from neo-Bauhaus to Mickey Mouse. The impact so galvanized Simms Taback, an illustrator familiar with the New York scene, that he determined to gather and show the best work of this New Illustration.

Tied to the rock and roll that beat between the album covers they illustrated, these artists clanged with energy. Booming off *Raw* magazine and laughing under the armpits of printed T-shirts, this stuff could not be denied. The Establishment didn't deny it; they just ignored it or seemed not to know it existed. Of course, some established art directors recognized a shift in ideology and many connected with the music industry did buy cover art or utilized the new sensibility in the pages of the *Rolling Stone*. But there was something missing.

To many, the Society of Illustrators Annual Exhibition represented the Establishment. There, art buyers, artists and students got a yearly dose of the best work being done in the country. Every art director had an Annual Book close at hand and used it as a Bible. Getting in the show generally meant getting work.

But a group of professionals—associates of Simms—felt the cross-section of work wasn't broad enough. They wanted to know why no one in their gang got in the show. As New York illustrator, Lou Brooks, put it: "We wanted to show that there were alternatives. That's not to say they're better or worse...Are you listening Bob Peak? It seems our group was more willing to accept both worlds. But the classic illustrator," he continued, "seemed to be intimidated."

Intimidation or lack of interest, it's unclear. It *was* true that the artists and art directors who made up the juries were not particularly attuned to these new artists. Though an occasional piece would slip into the Annual—Sue Coe, Barbara Nessim, for example, Simms felt that a whole show was necessary to give the sense of direction he felt was there. It was beyond Pushpin, which had acquired establishment status and it wasn't heavy social commentary. It was a different kind of energy; it had exuberance.

So he proposed a show of the "new look of American illustration" to the Board of Directors of the Society of Illustrators. From the onset, from every quarter, there was complete agreement that such a show should take place. The Society was not unaware of the criticism that existed. They were most willing, but they wanted to know what to expect. Not knowing what to expect himself, Simms could only give them a generic description: "A special show which will attempt to document a new direction in American illustration with special emphasis on the work of talented, younger, up-and-coming illustrators." It would be juried. A new Call for Entries list would be generated. Good publicity would be one of the rewards reaped. And perhaps a book.

Georganne Deen

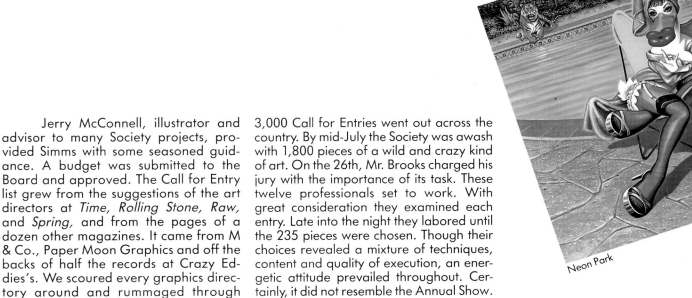

Neon Park

Jerry McConnell, illustrator and advisor to many Society projects, provided Simms with some seasoned guidance. A budget was submitted to the Board and approved. The Call for Entry list grew from the suggestions of the art directors at *Time, Rolling Stone, Raw,* and *Spring,* and from the pages of a dozen other magazines. It came from M & Co., Paper Moon Graphics and off the backs of half the records at Crazy Eddies's. We scoured every graphics directory around and rummaged through strange little shops in Soho and the East Village. And there was the very effective illustrators' grapevine.

Meanwhile, Simms had appointed as Jury Chairperson the crazed Lou Brooks with his airbrush and his whoopie cushion. It was through Lou that the invaluable L.A. connections were made. Mick Haggerty got to work on the art for a poster while Carol Carson, in New York, designed it. Lou and Simms assembled a dozen wise and just men and women whose heads slanted in the New direction.

At the Society two camps had been forming—both feeling the need for the show, but with differing opinions about the work Simms had been describing. The appearance of the Haggerty poster solidified these camps. As one observer remarked: ''Some thought this kind of art was absolute bullshit, poorly executed garbage. Others felt it was the new, the breakthrough, the necessary illustration.'' Tastes aside, they agreed that if Mick's work represented this ''New Illustration,'' the poster was valid.

It went to press and on June 7, 1982,

3,000 Call for Entries went out across the country. By mid-July the Society was awash with 1,800 pieces of a wild and crazy kind of art. On the 26th, Mr. Brooks charged his jury with the importance of its task. These twelve professionals set to work. With great consideration they examined each entry. Late into the night they labored until the 235 pieces were chosen. Though their choices revealed a mixture of techniques, content and quality of execution, an energetic attitude prevailed throughout. Certainly, it did not resemble the Annual Show.

On September 28th the New Illustration opened. Rather, it exploded! The Society had never seen anything like it. 500 guests jammed into the two galleries of the Museum of American Illustration. Gone were the wingtips and the pearls. In their place were '50s tuxedo jackets and sneakers, men with permed shoulder length hair and women shorn to baldness. No wine and cheese, no way. Instead, a buffet made of Hostess Twinkies, pink and blue Snowballs, Bazooka and penny candy, sprinkled with Trix...by eight o'clock not a fireball remained. Forget the flowers graciously placed. Why not Ken and Barbie (demurely draped) as artist and model? Skip the woodwind quartet. Give them the Three Stooges as fashion designers.

Art was mounted off kilter; Mick Haggerty's Wippo record was encased in lucite and hung at 90° from the wall and the 16 entries for Heaven were grouped together in the lower gallery. Bob Feldgus, then the art director for *Bananas* magazine, propped himself against the railing where he heard two of the more conservative guests exclaim in horrified tones:

11

Gary Panter

''They're Teee-shirts!!? They're Teeeee!!!!-Shirts!!!?!?!'' To everyone's regret, Divine, Joe Franklin and Tom Carvel (creator of Cookie Puss) were unable to attend, but the joint jumped until the staff turned out all the lights and considered locking the die hards in the gallery for the night.

The next day, when the Twinkie crumbs had been swept away, one had to ask oneself, ''Just what is this New Illustration?'' What are Montxo Algora's race cars doing flying over a Mondrian highway? Is Gary Panter's Picasso T-shirt homage or send up? Is Robert Risko truely the reincarnation of Ivo Pannaggi?

These artists have incorporated a roster of influences that swings from Impressionism to '60s brassiere ads. They have plundered Futurism and paid tribute to Marvel Comics. They have knelt down before Walter Gropius and satirized Surrealism. Then they've reversed it. The energy generated from this synthesis is enormous: it pops from the very eyesockets of John Holmstrom's ''In the Nuthouse #35,'' it screams from Willardson & White's stretched video head and splashes from Lou Brooks's erotic parody, ''The Wetter The Better.''

As these illustrators have gone through the grab bag of artistic influences they have rejected the accompanying philosophies. The technqiues of Kandinsky are not backed up by the tenents of Abstract Expressionism. The primary geometry of Mondrian serves as background but holds no vision that art could be the instrument to change the objective condition of human life. In the clear, high-tech approach of many of these works there are the ghosts of Moholy-Nagy and the Bauhaus, though there is no intention to proselytize the idea of mass consumption.

In fact, if there is a coherent philosophic overview, it is the unidealistic and very American world of the mass consumer. The iconization of ''the product'' by artists like Warhol, Lichtenstein, Hamilton and Rosenquist set the trend in illustration today. After the post-World War II ideals got dragged through the mud in Cambodia and our skies filled with acid rain, the notion of the American Dream could only be viewed as ironic.

The advertising images that sold the Dream are incorporated in the New Illustration as elemental parts of an ironic whole. The work is high-spirited social comment—the Dream shattered—in the form of the exploding cigar and with the strident push of crayola color. Any form of pop culture is fodder for the imagination: comic strips going as far back as Krazy Kat, matchbooks of the '40s, ads from *Popular Mechanics* of the '50s, Hirshfeld's caricatures of the '30s, Mr. Potato Head and all of *Mad* magazine.

Traditionally, American illustration has been the last to pick up on artistic trends. The general marketplace was hardly avant garde and illustrators, by trade, catered to that market place. New concepts and styles were funnelled down to most illustrators which created a homogeneous atmosphere acceptable to the mass audience.

The many influences of the New Illustrator, however, create a sieve-like effect producing a hodgepodge of styles. These styles are joined by a similar attitude of parodic, even manic disillusionment. If these artists are disturbed by the glaring inequities in the distribution of wealth, by the dissolution of basic family values or by the likelihood of world annihilation, they are not expressing it in the sombre palette of Depression art or in the effectively grim pen-and-ink drawings of *The New York Times* Op Ed page. They are shot full of energy and sticking their tongues out at the world.

From the '60s on, events conspired to prove that Father didn't know best: assassination after assassination, Kent State and Chicago, the lies of Lyndon and Trickie Dick. When they heard the pedestal crash, the generation that grew up on Ken Kesey and David Bowie decided that humor was the best way to react to the fall. So now Everett Peck slams his fat yellow Studebaker into a cop car and exclaims, "OOPS!" Jim Heimann's collage of a '50s scene portrays a perfect Mom radiating her goggled daughter with a sun lamp and thinks, "It's Heaven." Neon Park turns ducks into sex pots that ridicule the poses of Jayne Mansfield, while Georganne Deen deals with the same subject in "Pretty Naked Girls" by pushing toward the dark edges of punk surrealism.

Though these images, as illustration, must serve the client's needs; no matter how far they expand the limitations, more and more, the pieces exist on their own. Because of this and the marketing outlets which are now open to artists, such as greeting cards, T-shirts and shopping bags,

the work is no longer an accompaniment: the illustration is the message.

These artists are canny children who are unwilling to put on the suits and ties of grown-ups. In addition to their sophisticated techniques, they possess brush cuts, high top sneakers and a nose-thumbing sensibility. Somewhere between Beaver Cleaver and the Yuppies these artists have found a way of living and flourishing in the junkyard of consumerism. Many who are in this book are not only flourishing, they're mainstreaming.

Was it the New Illustration Exhibition that did it? Not completely—it was time, after all—but as Jerry McConnell said, "It's true that many art directors felt the work was more acceptable if it hung on the walls of the Society. As a breed they're not inclined to take chances...it's their asses on the line. The show made a lot of people aware. And we've made a point to get a broader-based selection of opinions on the jury."

Even though Lou Brooks does covers for *Fortune*, Michael Doret works for *Reader's Digest*, and Elwood Smith's lovely wobblies are on every billboard in town; we've got a way to go before IBM uses Gary Panter's "Buy or Die" method of marketing.

So hunker down in your La-Z-Boy, open a bottle of Yoo Hoo and enjoy The New Illustration.

**Jill Bossert,** New York, 1984

Mick Haggerty

John Holstrom

# COMMENTS

**Solicited commentary on the exhibition and the opening.**

Fresh from a trip to Mother Russia, **Simms Taback** arrived just in time for opening night. His comment: "It's jumping off the walls!"

Photo: Woolworth's

"There really is something new going on here. A lot of the illustrators have taken what I find so difficult to deal with in recent times—the aggression, the fragmentation, the superficiality—and made dramatic, witty art out of it. The persistent optimism of the show was infectious, but I got over it."

**James McMullan**
illustrator/author

Photo: Jeffrey Smith

Along with the inauguration in 1981 of the Society of Illustrators Museum of American Illustration was the recognition of its commitment to exhibit all forms of the art of illustration. The "New Illustration" exhibition was a reflection of that commitment.

Among the membership, the professional and student communities, and the interested public, it created controversy, inspiration and much thought.

That, it seems, is the purpose of all art and the primary obligation of every museum.

**John Witt**
President of the Society of Illustrators, 1980-83

Photo: Playland

"Years ago we got tired of submitting and none of us ever getting in. If one of us did, it was a fluke...or a flounder. Now I'm so mainstream I just bought a White Westinghouse washer-dryer."

**Lou Brooks**
illustrator

Illustration: Sam Viviano

14

The title ''The New Illustration'' is to my way of thinking somewhat of a misnomer. But in the end it may be the best way of wrapping up and defining the diverse attitudes and styles contained in the show and book.

I say misnomer because, after all, there is nothing really new here. Illustration—or art for that matter—is a continuous process of taking bits and pieces from the past, tossing them around in our minds and spewing out something fresh. It's kind of like teaching an old dog new tricks. This art doesn't represent something that just bloomed overnight. The history of illustration shows us that there has always been a ''new illustration''. There has always been someone who was willing to test the limits of the conventional and then take the risk in going beyond. If there wasn't a ''new illustration'' then art itself would stagnate and die. I hope that because of shows and books like this the attitude and energies represented here will become part of the established and accepted norm. Of course, this will foster a certain amount of complacency and force into battle a whole new batch of emerging artists. They will then brandish the banner of ''The 'New' New Illustration''. And so on, ad infinitum.

**Michael Doret**
graphic designer/illustrator

Illustration: Laura Smith

Exaggerated, stylistic expressionism is a concise way to explain the New Illustration that's being done today. Its fresh personal style seems to have more to do with expressing one's own views in context with that of the subject.

**Barbara Nessim**
illustrator

Photo: Seiji Kakizaki

I first started to use the ''new illustration'' in *Bananas* in the mid-'70s. I was aware, not of a trend, but of the fact that ''regular'' or ''old'' illustration and photography was not right for my audience (young teenagers). The visuals for them had to be more complete. Therefore, a more design-oriented approach was needed—illustration closely related and actually created with typography and graphic design elements.

Gradually, I used the ''new illustration'' for the other products I was art directing: book covers, posters, text books, etc. Over the years the ''new illustrators'' and the ''traditional'' ones came to be viewed as two completely

different species. The work of the ''new'' was not being shown in Society Annuals and resentment was growing. It was unfortunate because, for me, *all* forms of illustration are valid. Also, I knew from experience that the ''new illustrators'' were as dedicated, serious and professional as any.

The show at the Society helped to heal *some* of the wound, although I'm sure that it shocked and outraged many ''old liners,'' which *is* really unfortunate.

**Bob Feldgus**
free-lance art director

Illustration: Sam Viviano

"I LOVED THE OPENING!"
**Robert Risko,** illustrator

Photo: David Hartman

"The best of it is an attempt to stretch things to the limit within the boundaries of illustration, which, by definition, requires the satisfaction of the client. The goal is to convince the client that images produced with a new attitude and with new technologies can serve his needs."

**Mick Haggerty**
illustrator, from Graphis 224/1983 - Graphis Press Corp., Zurich, Switzerland

Illustration: Mick Haggerty

If this is the "new" illustration, what is the rest of the work in the Society's shows to be called? "Old"? "Establishment"?

It is very important to create a real climate of opinion within the Society and amongst jury members such that *any* work can be submitted to the Annual show and have a fighting chance of being *selected*, not just tolerated for the sake of a paternal nod in the "new" direction.

Illustrations of all types are appearing in newspapers, magazines and books, on posters, film and tv. Only in the context of everything else can this "new" work be seen for what it is worth. By holding a separate show, the Society made a statement about the quality of both the "new" and the "other" work, that was detrimental to each one.

But progress has been made, and some of the pieces that have started to appear in the Annual since the New Illustration show are a testament to the flexibility of an organization that was once thought to be a bastion of only the more traditional forms. Keep up the good, "new", work!

**Nigel Holmes**
Executive Art Director, Time Magazine

Photo: Debbie Wells

"Like all movements, some of it was innovative, but a lot of the stuff was trendy and meaningless."

**Marvin Mattelson**
illustrator

Illustration: Marvin Mattelson

R. TIBOR KALMAN

"Hey, it's art!"
**Tibor Kalman**
graphic designer

Illustration: Maira Berman

"Judging the New Illustration Show was a little bit of a vindication. Rejecting the evaluation process that most art directors use, I looked for bold, strong design that could stand on its own as art, that's all. For once, who cared if it was suitable or not, or understandable?

Naturally, many of my favorites were pieces that had been killed. Dead drawings have greatness that comes from having suffered!

Illustrators need more chances like this show and book to let the public see what some editor or publisher felt was in some way below, or above, or beyond the public's understanding."

**Laurie Rosenwald**
graphic designer/illustrator

Photo: Howard Read

It was a party.
A "bust out" to be more
    accurate.
It was loud, rude, serious,
    irreverent,
slapstick and fun.
In concert all those different
    voices generated
a visual shout that excited
    and stimulated as
few shows of this kind have
    ever done.
"New Illustration" had an
    energy of
expression so direct, volatile
and physical that it worked
because it just didn't feel
like work.
It was a terrific party.

**Doug Johnson**
illustrator

Photo: Anne Leigh

It was so important to have the Society of Illustrators produce a breakthrough show of the New Progressive Illustrators (better known as The Progs). By the excitement generated at the opening night, it was obvious that "we had arrived" in our field of communication, a field so much in need of unique, fresh approaches and techniques. I was honored and proud to be included in this show. The feedback was more than I expected: it stimulated and encouraged. New doors have blown open that will never close.

**Ron Lieberman**
illustrator/designer

Photo: Nancy Stevenson

**Ron Lieberman**
for Duval/Leigh and
Because Productions

**Lou Beach**
Art Director: Roger
Carpenter for Oui

**Mike Fink**
Art Director: Ron Coro
for Elektra/Asylum Records

this page
**Christopher Hopkins**
for Dumas Studios

opposite above
**Kathy Staico Schorr**
Art Director: Brad Benedict
for Heaven

opposite below
**Todd Schorr**
for Heaven

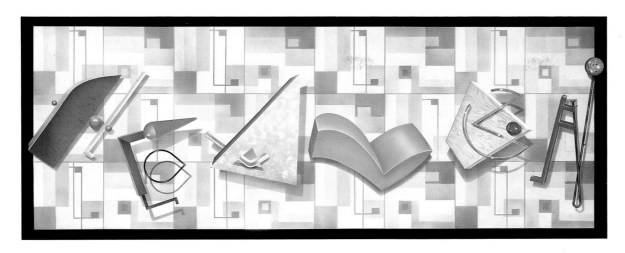

**Kako Nakamori**

**Kit Grover**
Art Director: Carin Goldberg
for CBS Records

**Montxo Algora**
for Dos I Una

**Bob Zoell**
Art Director: Brad Benedict
for Heaven

this page
**Michael Doret**
Art Directors Irene Ramp
and Michael Doret
for Peregrine, Inc.

24

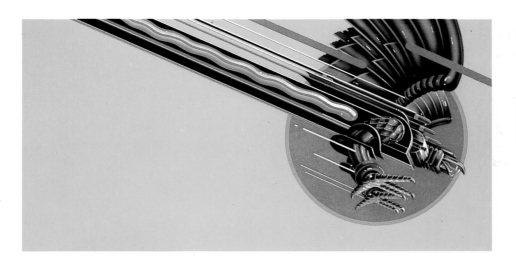

above left
**Doug Johnson**
Art Director: John Berg
for CBS Records

below left
**Michael Doret**
Art Director: Dennis Woloch of
Howard Marks Advertising Inc.
for Casablanca Records

right
**Jim Cherry III**
Art Director: John Workman
for Heavy Metal Magazine

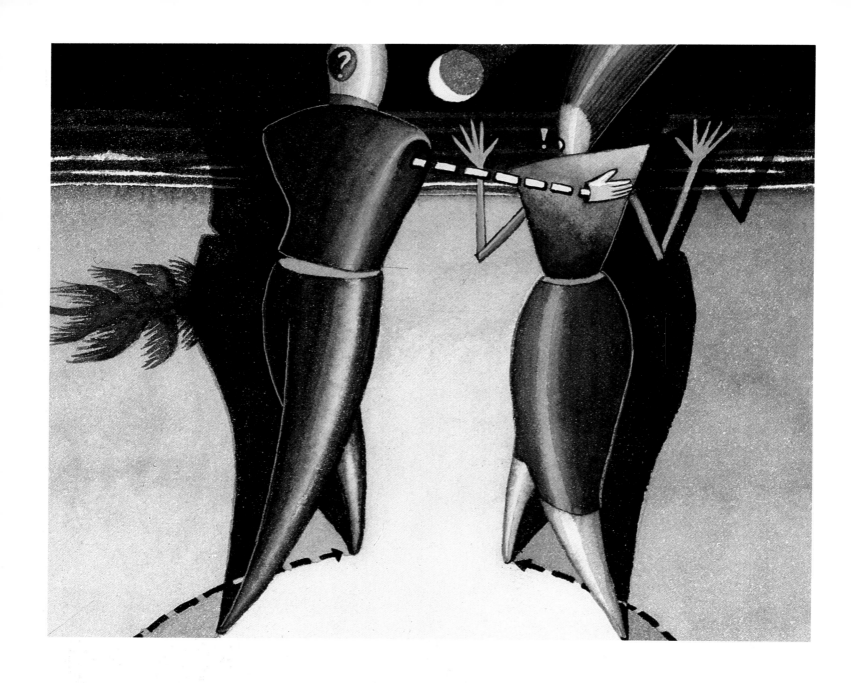

**Barry Root**
Art Director: Dan Lloyd
Taylor for Savvy Magazine

**Georganne Deen**
Art Director: Peter Wolf
for EMI Liberty

# THE J. GEILS BAND

*Freeze-Frame*

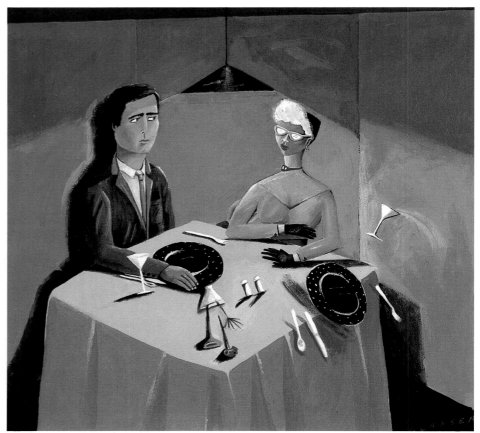

**John Holmstrom**　　　　　　　　　**Judy Glasser**

**Cynthia Marsh**
for Davis-Blue Artworks

**Kuniyasu Hashimoto**
Art Director: Jane Ethe
for Allied Graphic Arts

**Robert Risko**
for Brad Benedict

**Clive Piercy**
for Hot Seat Furniture

**Lou Brooks**
Art Director: Peter Nevraumont
for Ruby Street

**Charles White III**
for Portal Publications

"AST YEAR, recruiters from the industrial plants of America flocked to colleges to obtain what money could not buy—enough engineers."

above
**Robert Kopecky**

below
**Judy Glasser**
Art Director: Rostislav Elsmont
for Chief Executive Magazine

right
**Gary Panter**
Art Director: Walter Bernard
for Time Magazine

**John Craig**
Art Director: Bob Ungar
for Passages Magazine

**Elwood H. Smith**
Art Director: David Rollert
for Dell Publishing

**Sue Llewellyn**
Art Directors: Mary Zisk
and Frank Rothmann
for Science Digest

left
**Joel Resnicoff**
for Illustration Magazine

right
**Mike Fink**
Art Director: Brad Benedict
for Heaven

opposite above
**Mark Newgarden**

left
**Tommy Steele**
for The Sights

above left
**Bob Zoell**
for Heaven

above right
**Mick Haggerty**
for Heaven

below left
**Jim Heimann**
for Heaven

below right
**Laurie Rosenwald**
for Heaven

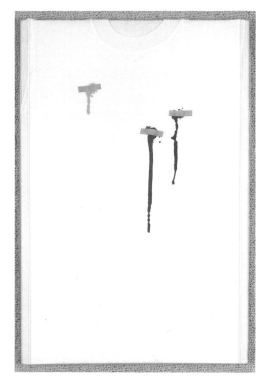

above left
**Everett Peck**
for Heaven

above right
**Tommy Steele**
for Heaven

below left
**Gary Panter**
for Heaven

below right
**Mike Fink**
for Heaven

**Paul Rogers**

**Mick Haggerty**
Art Director: Ron Coro
for Elektra/Asylum Records

**Karen M. McDonald**

**Cathy Barancik**
Art Director: David Brown
for Dayton's

**Cathy Barancik**
Art Director: Larry Jennings
for Bergdorf Goodman

opposite above
**Lucinda Cowell**
Art Director: Roger
Carpenter for Paper Moon
Graphics

opposite below
**Syd Daniels**

above
**Lou Beach**
Art Director: Jeff Ayeroff
for A & M Records

**Lou Brooks**
Art Director: Brad Benedict

**Tim Clark**
Art Director: Sandi Silbert
for East/West Network

**Lou Brooks/Todd Schorr**
Art Director: Bob Feldgus
for Scholastic Book Service

above
**Rhonda Voo**
Art Director: Don Dame
for Windemere Press

opposite above left
**Joel Resnicoff**
for Intercoiffure

opposite above right
**Sue Llewellyn**

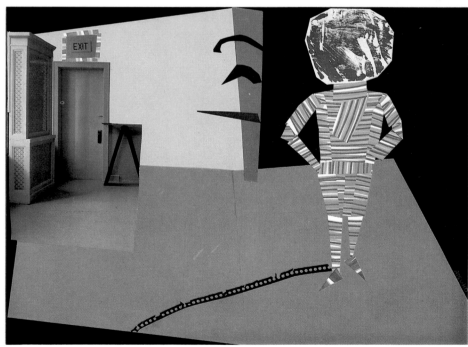

left
**Atsuko Shimizu**

Heimann

**Jim Heimann**
Art Director: Allyson Rowen
for Decorative Carpets, Inc.

**Jim Heimann**
for Peter Shire Pottery

**Laurie Rosenwald**
Art Director: Bea Feitler
for Vanity Fair

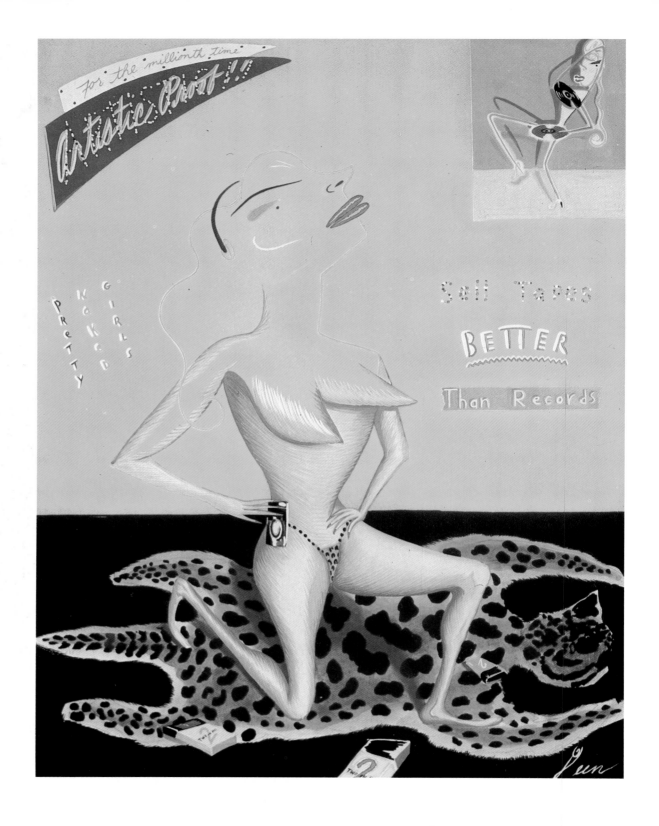

**Georganne Deen**
Art Director: Rick Seirini
For Warner Bros.

**John O'Leary**
Art Director: Paula Scher
for CBS Records

above
**Montxo Algora**
for On/Safia

below
**Frank Olinsky**

opposite
**Bob Barancik**

opposite above
**Jim Heimann**
Art Director: Brad Benedict
for Heaven

opposite below
**Dave McMacken**
Art Director: Brad Benedict
for Heaven

below
**Jim Heimann**
Art Director: Brad Benedict
for Heaven

**Michael Emerson**
Art Director: Russell Zolan
for Science Digest

**Kurt Vargo**
Art Director: Jeffrey Saks
for Art Direction Magazine

**Barton E. Stabler**
Art Director: Don Weller

Side 1

Happy Man

Every Love Song

Everyday/Saturday

Dedication

Tell Me Lies

Side 2

Testify

Sound System

Seeing Is Believing

Higher And Higher

Family

Greg Kihn

Larry Lynch

Gary Phillips

Steve Wright

Dave Carpender

PRODUCED BY Matthew King Kaufman
ENGINEERED BY Dr. Schnaz
ASSISTANT ENGINEER Gary Mobish
LEAD VOCALS ON HIGHER AND HIGHER BY Larry Lynch
MASTERED BY George Horn
RECORDED AT Fantasy Studio, Berkeley, California
ART DIRECTION Ron Coro
ART + DESIGN Mike Fink
PHOTOGRAPHY Kaz Tsuruta

GREG KIHN BAND

KIHNTINUED

above
**Mike Fink**
Art Director: Ron Coro
for Elektra/Asylum Records

below left
**Mark Andresen**
Art Director: Sara Seine
for Brown's Guide to Georgia

below right
**Everett Peck**
Art Director: Elizabeth Kooker
for Mark Taper Forum

above
**Steven Guarnaccia**
Art Director: Chris Austopchuk
for Rolling Stone

**Mick Haggerty**

**Lou Brooks**
Art Director: Charles Riddell
for Northern Ohio Live

**Daniel Kirk**
Art Director: Norman Oberlander
for Swank Magazine

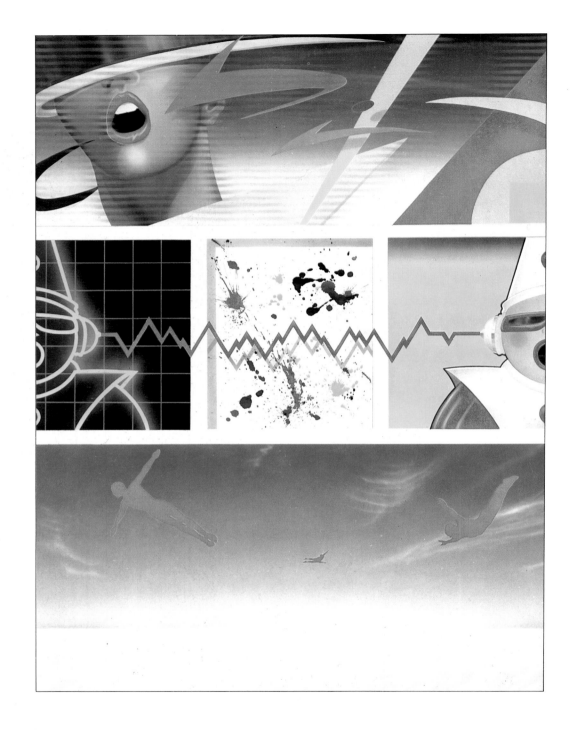

above
**Montxo Algora**
for Heavy Metal Magazine

*FAME* IS THE ARTISTS:

Charles E. White III

John Van Hamersveld

David Edward Byrd

David Willardson

Robert Grossman

George Stavrinos

Richard Amsel

Cynthia Marsh

Doug Johnson

Andy Warhol

Neon Park

Antonio

and others

*FAME* IS THE FAMOUS:

Elvis

Blondie

The Who

Sissy Spacek

Woody Allen

Dolly Parton

Steve Martin

Raquel Welch

Jimmy Carter

Paul McCartney

Marilyn Monroe

Humphrey Bogart

and more

Brad Benedict

F A M E

ISBN:0-517-541610

Brad Benedict · Portraits of Celebrated People

above
**Richard Bernstein**
Art Director: Brad Benedict
for Harmony Books

below left
**Montxo Algora**
for Heavy Metal Magazine

below right
**Pater Sato**
Art Director: Kenkichi Harada
for Vox Gallery

**Susan Bannon**

**Julia Gorton**

**Eugène Mihaesco**
Art Director: Rudolph Hoglund
for Time Magazine

**Mick Haggerty**
for Brad Benedict

**Christopher Hopkins**
Art Director: Charles White III
for Margarethe Hubauer

**April Greiman**
Art Directors: Adam Sommers
and April Greiman
for Warner Bros. Records

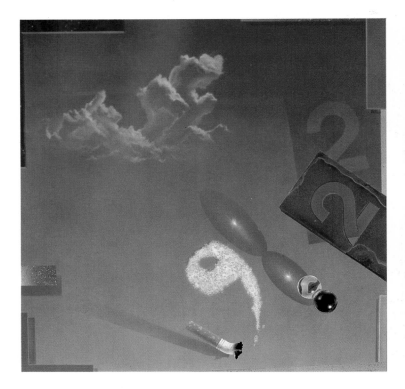

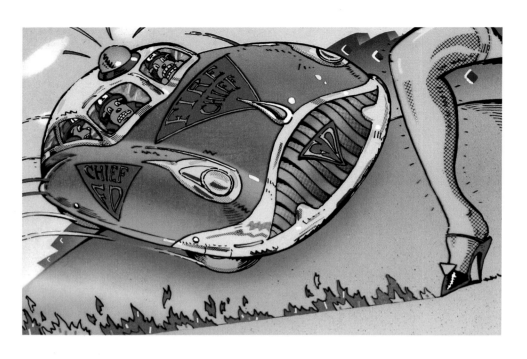

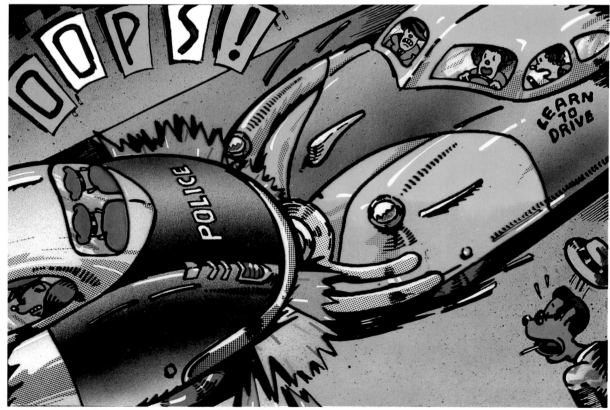

opposite above
**Everett Peck**
for Brad Benedict

opposite below
**Everett Peck**
for Look Out!

above
**John Van Hamersveld**
Art Director: Brad Benedict
for Heaven

above left
**Michael Doret**
Art Director: Walter Bernard
for Time Magazine

above right
**Michael Doret**
for Seibundo-Shinkosha
Publishing Company

below
**Steven M. Singer**
Art Director: Woody Pirtle
for ''D'' Magazine

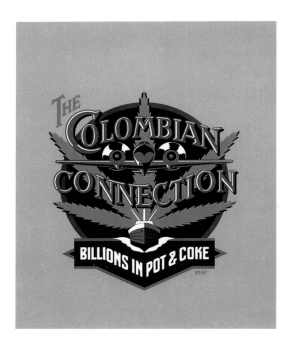

below
**Gary Panter**
for Warner Bros. Records

right
**Georganne Deen**
Art Director: Jules Bates
for A & M Records

above
**Robert Kopecky**

below
**Barbara Nessim**
Art Director: Paula Greif
for Mademoiselle

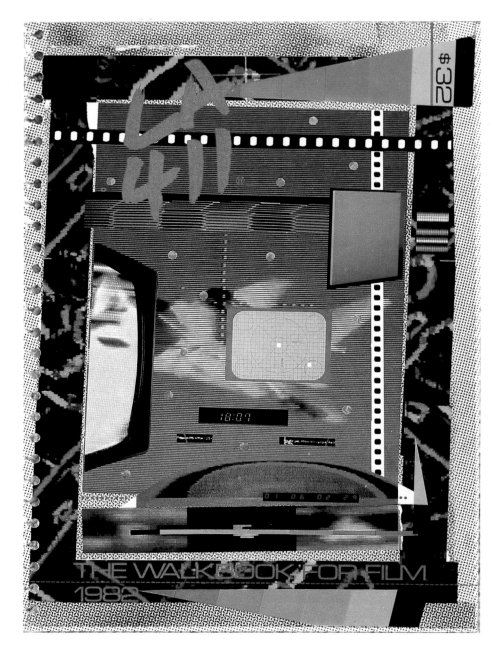

**Lou Beach**
for L.A. 411

**Jim Heimann**
Art Director: Fred Roses
for Easy Aces

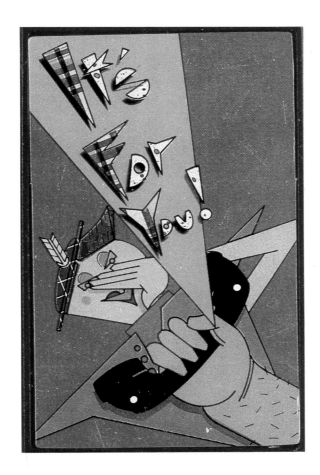

**Jim Heimann**
Art Director: Fred Roses
for Easy Aces

**Jim Cherry III**
for Universe Press

**Steve Carver**
Art Director: R. Wayne Kruse
for Theatre Theater

**Beatrice Fassell**
Art Director: Louise Fili
for Random House

**Wendy L. Burden**
for Heaven

80

**John O'Leary**
Art Director: Paula Scher
for CBS Records

**Mark Andresen**

**Ron Lieberman**
for Warner Bros. Records

**Ron Lieberman**
for Warner Bros. Records

**Dave Calver**
Art Director: Greg Paul
for Ohio Plain Dealer Magazine

left
**Mike Fink**
Art Director: Brad Benedict
for Heaven

right
**Mike Fink**
Art Director: Brad Benedict
for Heaven

above
**Mike Fink**
Art Director: Brad Benedict
for Heaven

below
**Gary Panter**
Art Director: Brad Benedict
for Heaven

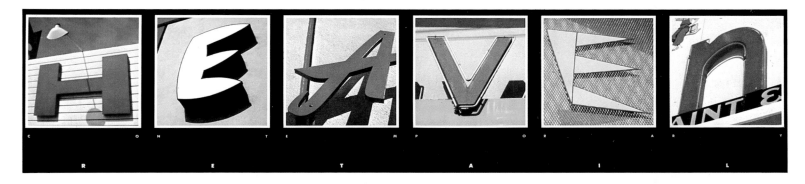

**Maira Berman**

**Georganne Deen**
Art Director: Paula Scher
for CBS Records

**Lou Beach**
Art Director: Roland Young
for A & M Records

**Anders Wenngren**
Art Director: Karen Brown
for Dayton's

**Laurie Rosenwald**
Art Director: Bea Feitler
for Vanity Fair

**Kathy Staico Schorr**
Art Director: Roger
Carpenter for Paper Moon
Graphics

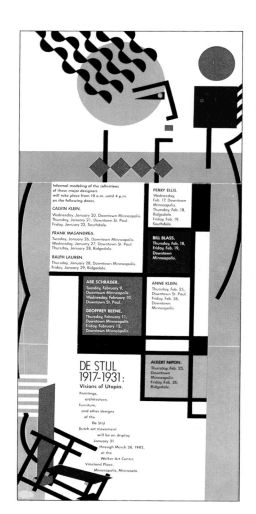

**Chad Draper**

**Cathy Barancik**
Art Director: Andrew J. Epstein
for Moviegoer Magazine

90

**Leslie Carbaga**
Art Directors: Rudolph Hoglund
and Nigel Holmes
for Time Magazine

**Jim Cherry III**
for Heavy Metal Magazine

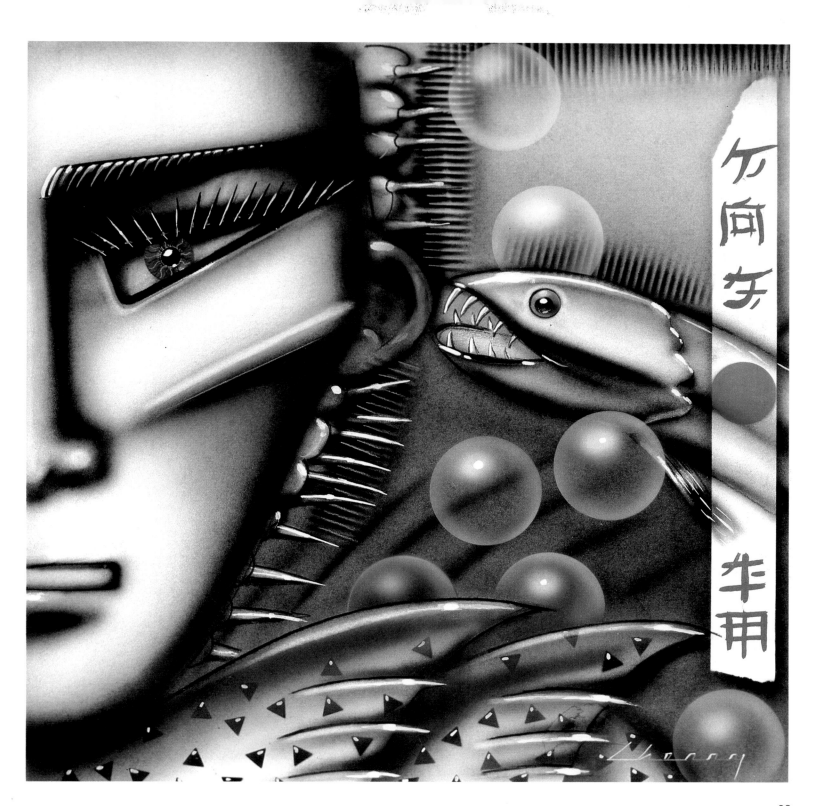

**Paul Davis**
Art Director: Reinhold Schwenk
for New York Shakespeare
Festival

**Marshall Arisman**
Art Director: Rudolph Hoglund
for Time Magazine

**Mark Falls**

**Renée Klein**
Art Director: Katy Aldrich
for The Boston Globe

95

above left
**Seymour Chwast**
for Push Pin Graphic

above right
**N.A. Kintisch**
Art Director: Hiroku Tanaka
for Illustration Magazine

below
**N. A. Kintisch**
Art Director: Lester Goodman
for Family Health Magazine

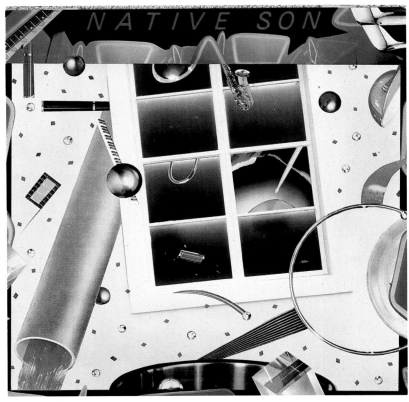

**April Greiman/Jayme Odgers**
for Douglas Schmidt

**Lou Beach**
Art Director: Pat McGowan
for Infinity Records

**Charles White III**
Art Director: Chuck Besan
for A & M Records

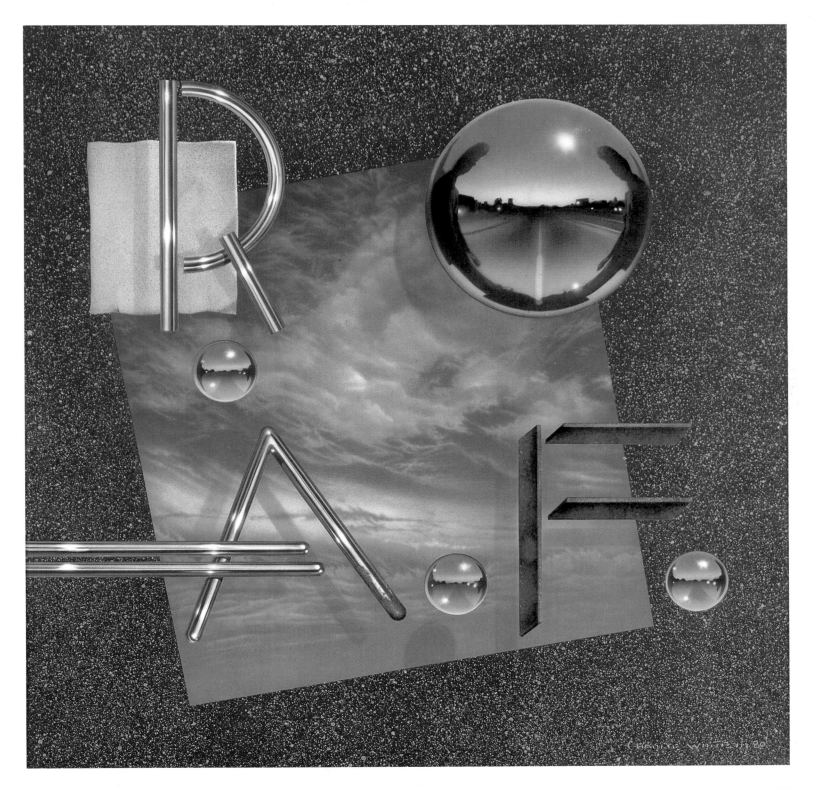

above left
**Gary Panter**
for Heaven

above right
**Lou Brooks**
for Heaven

below left
**Lou Brooks**
for Heaven

below right
**Michael Doret**
for Heaven

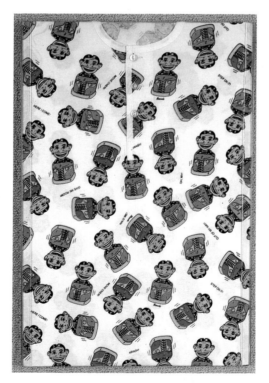

above left
**Gary Panter**
Art Director: Pee-Wee Herman
for Heaven

below left
**Robert Risko**
for Heaven

above right
**Bob Zoell**
for Heaven

**Bob Rose**

**Robert Kopecky**

**Jim Heimann**
for Look Out!

PARADING POOLSIDE POODLES
THREATENED BY MAD
CHIHUAHUA

above
**Mark Marek**
for National Lampoon

opposite above
**Gary Panter**
for Warner Bros. Records

opposite below
**Gary Panter**
for Ralph Records

**Elwood H. Smith**
Art Director: David Rollert
for Dell Publishing

**Robert Risko**
for Brad Benedict

**Mark Andresen**
Art Director: Peter Hudson
for Atlanta Magazine

**Renée Klein**
Art Director: Lynn Staley
for The Boston Globe

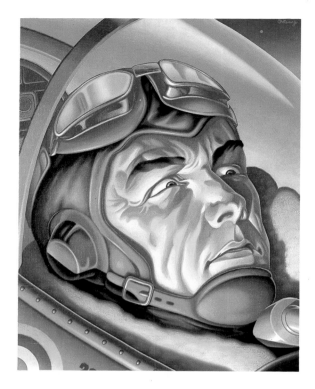

THE LUDLUM SECRET

opposite above
**John O'Leary**
Art Director: Bob Feldgus
for Scholastic Book Service

opposite below
**John O'Leary**
Art Director: Tom Lulevitch
for US Air Magazine

above
**Georganne Deen**

**Robert Risko**
Art Director: Bea Feitler
for Vanity Fair

**Montxo Algora**

above
**Jeanne Fisher**

below
**Jim Heimann**
Art Director: Andre Sota
for Portal Publications

left
**Kurt Vargo**

right
**Anders Wenngren**
Art Director: Pegi Goodman
for Rolling Stone

ADVANCED
ELECTRONICS

# HI-FI TO GO
## A GUIDE TO PERSONAL STEREO

STEPHEN A. BOOTH

**Jim Cherry III**
Art Director: Helen Hall
for Ralph Records

**Montxo Algora**

**Mark Andresen**
Art Director: Peter Hudson
for Technology Illustrated
Magazine

**Elwood H. Smith**
Art Director: Chris Austopchuk
for Rolling Stone

**Gary Panter**
for Ralph Records

**Steven M. Singer**

**Lou Brooks**
Art Director: Bob Feldgus
for Scholastic Book Service

**Jim Heimann**
for Peter Shire Pottery

**Doug Taylor**
Art Director: Peter Nevraumont
for Ruby Street

left
**Jeanne Fisher**
Art Directors: Bea Feitler
and Janet Perr
for Rolling Stone

right
**Leslie Carbaga**
Art Director: Sandi Young
for Atlantic Records

above
**Mike Fink**
Art Director: Brad Benedict
for Heaven

below
**Jim Heimann**
Art Director: Brad Benedict
for Heaven

above
**Barbara Nessim**
Art Director: Shinichiro Tora
for Hotel Barmen's Association
of Japan

below
**Green/DeLancie**

opposite
**Green/Delancie**
for Art Direction Magazine

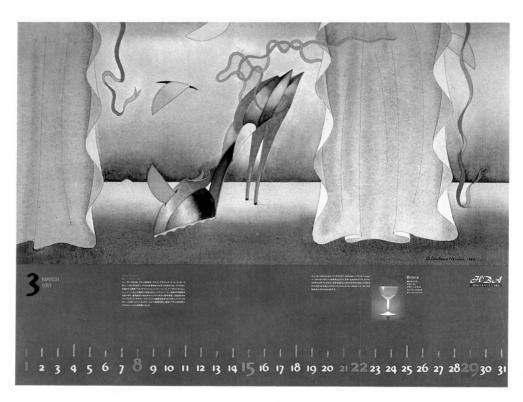

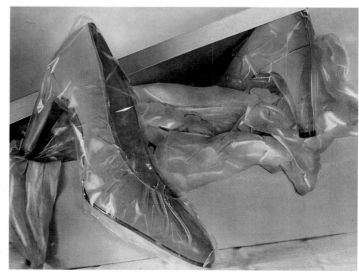

122

above
**Stan Watts**

opposite above
**Jim Wilson/Carl Waltzer**
Art Director: Jim Wilson
for Playboy Magazine

opposite below
**David Willardson/
Charles White III**
Art Director: Camiel Lane
for Universal Studio

Christmas At Mr. Bill's

Cutting the Tree

Wrapping Presents

Caroling

Santa Arrives

Making Eggnog

*in the spirit of the season, playboy presents your favorite superhero*

Playing with His New Toys

Christmas Finally Ends

Cooking Christmas Dinner

Created and Produced by Walter Williams
Graphics, Sets and Models by Jim Wilson
Photography by Carl Waltzer

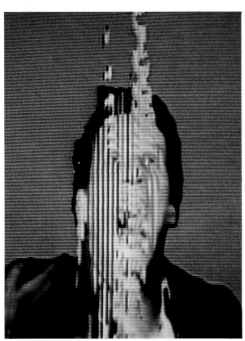

**Neon Park**
for Warner Bros. Records

**John O'Leary**
Art Director: Greg Scott
for Rolling Stone

**Pater Sato**
for Parco Publishing, Inc.

**Scott Neary**
Art Director: Stephen Doyle
for Rolling Stone

**Robert Risko**
Art Director: Robert Hayes
for Interview

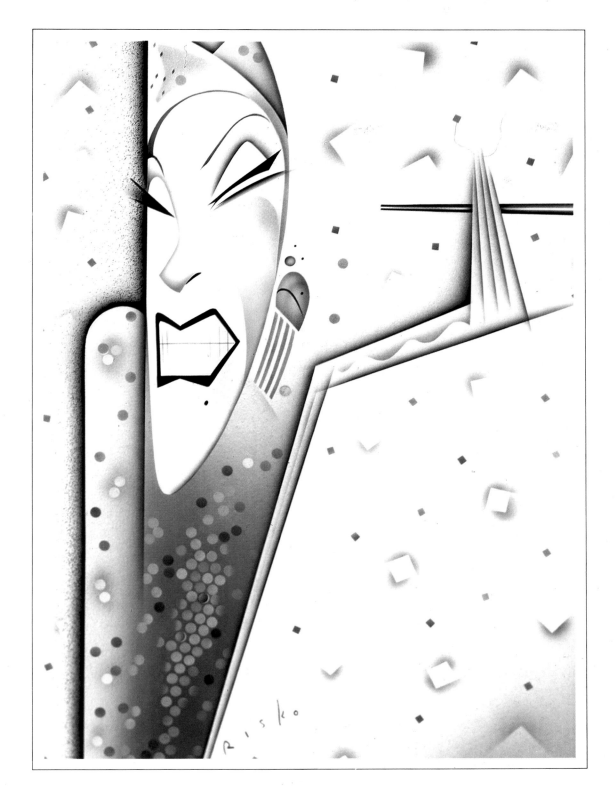

opposite above
**Tim Clark**
Art Director: Leslie Barnett
for Emmy Magazine

opposite below
**Michael Doret**
Art Director: Rudolph Hoglund
for Time Magazine

above
**Michael Doret**
Art Director: John Jay
for Bloomingdale's

above
**Laurie Rosenwald**
Art Director: Brian Burdine
for Bloomingdale's

below
**April Greiman/
Jayme Odgers**
for California Institute of the Arts

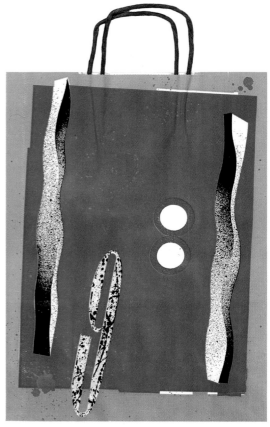

left
**Jeanne Fisher**
for The New York Times

right
**Michael Doret**
Art Director: Walter Bernard
for Time Magazine

left
**Dave McMacken**
Art Director: Ron Coro
for CBS Records

above right
**Mark Falls**

below right
**Karen M. McDonald**

left
**Marshall Arisman**
Art Director: Walter Bernard
for Time Magazine

**Renée Klein**
Art Director: Ronn Campisi
for The Boston Globe

**Mark Newgarden**

**Elwood H. Smith**
Art Director: Yoshihisa Ishihara
for Idea Magazine

**Don Ivan Punchatz**
Art Director: Byron Preiss
for Baronet Publishing

**Don Ivan Punchatz**
Art Director: Byron Preiss
for Baronet Publishing

**Robert Kopecky**

F e s t i v a l
**of Festivals**

The 7th Annual
International Film Festival

Toronto
September 9-18, 1982

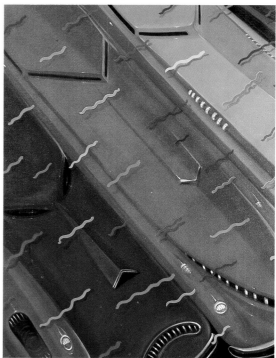

**Bill Mayer**

**Bill Mayer**
Art Director: Dan Taylor
for Playboy Enterprises, Inc.

**Karen M. McDonald**

**Barbara Nessim**
Art Directors: Mare Early
and Barbara Nessim
for Scarlett Letters

**Elwood H. Smith**
Art Directors: Richard Wilde
and Bill Kobasz
for School of Visual Arts

**Susan Cohen**
Art Director: Pamela Vassil
for The New York Times

**Robert Risko**
Art Director: Andrew J. Epstein
for Moviegoer Magazine

146

**Lou Brooks**
for Heaven

**Jim Heimann**
for Heaven

**Michael Doret**
for Heaven

THE MULTIPLE NEEDS OF YOUR DOG

**Robert Kopecky**

**Laurie Rosenwald**
Art Director: David Bowie
for RCA

**Michael Doret**
for Look Out!

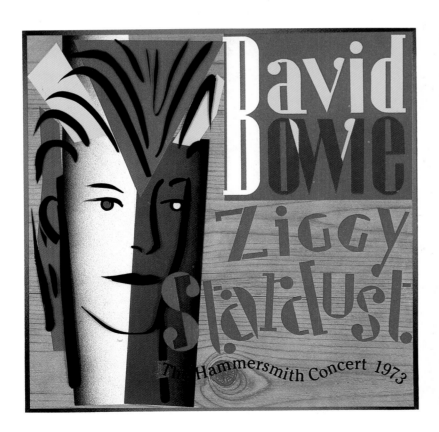

above
**Lou Brooks**
Art Director: Bob Feldgus
for Scholastic Book Service

opposite above
**Mick Haggerty**
Art Director: Jeff Ayeroff
for Man Made Records

opposite below
**Joel Resnicoff**
for Yoshi Inaba/Bigi Co., Ltd.

**Brad Holland**
Art Directors: Paul Hardy
and Miles Abernathy
for Attenzione Magazine

**Cynthia Marsh**
Art Director: Mike Fink
for Laurian Beyer and
Christoper Lagget

**Ken Krug**

**Todd Schorr**
Art Directors: Richard Schaefer
and Paul Zalon
for PopShots, Inc.

**Doug Taylor**
Art Director: Peter Nevraumont
for Ruby Street

**Randall Enos**
Art Director: Chris Austopchuk
for Rolling Stone Magazine

above
**Vivienne Flesher**
Art Director: Irene Ramp
for Time Magazine

opposite above
**Karen M. McDonald**

opposite below
**Keiji Obata**

**Doug Taylor**
Art Director: Paula Scher
for CBS Records

**Doug Taylor**
Art Director: Bob Feldgus
for Scholastic Book Service

158

Algora, Montxo 23, 54, 64, 65, 111, 115
Andresen, Mark 60, 81, 107, 115
Arisman, Marshall 94, 135
Bannon, Susan 66
Barancik, Bob 55
Barancik, Cathy 43, 91
Bernstein, Richard 65
Berman, Maira 86
Beach, Lou 18, 45, 76, 87, 98
Brooks, Lou 31, 46, 47, 63, 100, 118, 146, 150
Burden, Wendy L. 79
Carbaga, Leslie 92, 120
Calver, Dave 83
Carver, Steve 78
Cherry III, Jim 25, 77, 93, 114
Chwast, Seymour 97
Clark, Tim 46, 130
Cohen, Susan 145
Cowell, Lucinda 44
Craig, John 34
Daniels, Syd 44
Davis, Paul 94
Georganne Deen 27, 52, 74, 87, 109
Doret, Michael 24, 25, 72, 100, 130, 131, 133, 147, 149

Draper, Chad 90
Emerson, Michael 58
Enos, Randall 155
Falls, Mark 95, 134
Fassell, Beatrice 78
Fink, Mike 19, 36, 39, 60, 84, 85, 96, 121
Fisher, Jeanne 112, 120, 133
Flesher, Vivienne 156
Glasser, Judy 28, 33
Gorton, Julia 66
Green/deLancie 122, 123
Greiman, April 69, 98, 132
Grover, Kit 22
Guarnaccia, Steven 61
Haggerty, Mick 38, 41, 62, 68, 151
Hashimoto, Kuniyasu 29
Heimann, Jim 38, 50, 51, 56, 57, 76, 77, 103, 112, 119, 121, 147
Holland, Brad 152
Holmstrom, John 28
Hopkins, Christopher 20, 69
Johnson, Doug 25
Klein, Renée 95, 107, 136
Kintisch, N.A. 97
Kirk, Daniel 63, 141

Kopecky, Robert 33, 75, 102, 139, 148
Krug, Ken 153
Lieberman, Ron 18, 82
Llewellyn, Sue 35, 49
Marek, Mark 104
Marsh, Cynthia 29, 153
Mayer, Bill 142
McDonald, Karen M. 42, 134, 143, 157
McMacken, Dave 56, 134
Mihaesco, Eugene 67
Nakamori, Kako 22
Neary, Scott 128
Nessim, Barbara 75, 122, 144
Newgarden, Mark 37, 137
Obata, Keiji 157
Odgers, Jayme 98, 132, 140
O'Leary, John 53, 80, 108, 127
Olinsky, Frank 54
Panter, Gary 33, 39, 73, 85, 100, 101, 105, 116
Park, Neon 126
Peck, Everett 39, 60, 70
Piercy, Clive 31
Punchatz, Don Ivan 138
Resnicoff, Joel 36, 49, 151
Risko, Robert 30, 101, 106, 110,

129, 145
Rogers, Paul 40
Root, Barry 26
Rose, Bob 102
Rosenwald, Laurie 38, 51, 88, 132, 149
Sato, Pater 65, 127
Schorr, Kathy Staico 21, 89
Schorr, Todd 21, 47, 141, 154
Shimizu, Atsuko 49
Singer, Steven M. 72, 117
Smith, Elwood H. 34, 106, 116, 137, 144
Stabler, Barton E. 59
Steele, Tommy 37, 39
Taylor, Doug 119, 154, 158
Van Hamersveld, John 71
Vargo, Kurt 59, 113
Voo, Rhonda 48
Waltzer, Carl 125
Watts, Stan 124
Wenngren, Anders 88, 113
White III, Charles 32, 99, 125
Willardson, David 125
Wilson, Jim 125
Zoell, Bob 23, 38, 101